CAMBRIDGE LIBRARY COLLECTION

Books of enduring scholarly value

Cambridge

The city of Cambridge received its royal charter in 1201, having already been home to Britons, Romans and Anglo-Saxons for many centuries. Cambridge University was founded soon afterwards and celebrated its octocentenary in 2009. Th is series explores the history and influence of Cambridge as a centre of science, learning, and discovery, its contributions to national and global politics and culture, and its inevitable controversies and scandals..

College Life

These 'letters to an undergraduate' were published in 1845, two years after the death of their author, Thomas Whytehead (1815–43). His outstanding student career at Cambridge suggested that he would remain in academic life, but having been ordained deacon and then priest, he volunteered for missionary work, and in 1841 sailed for the southern hemisphere as chaplain to the newly appointed Bishop Selwyn. He became seriously ill on arrival in Australia, and died in New Zealand the following year. This work was created during Whytehead's time as a curate, and later on his travels: he felt strongly that new undergraduates at Oxford and Cambridge should have a spiritual and moral guide to life in college as well as a history of university institutions and customs. The letters cover the collegiate system, discipline, rooms, the chapel and hall, the lecture room and library, and the lasting importance of college friends.

Cambridge University Press has long been a pioneer in the reissuing of out-of-print titles from its own backlist, producing digital reprints of books that are still sought after by scholars and students but could not be reprinted economically using traditional technology. The Cambridge Library Collection extends this activity to a wider range of books which are still of importance to researchers and professionals, either for the source material they contain, or as landmarks in the history of their academic discipline.

Drawing from the world-renowned collections in the Cambridge University Library and other partner libraries, and guided by the advice of experts in each subject area, Cambridge University Press is using state-of-the-art scanning machines in its own Printing House to capture the content of each book selected for inclusion. The files are processed to give a consistently clear, crisp image, and the books finished to the high quality standard for which the Press is recognised around the world. The latest print-on-demand technology ensures that the books will remain available indefinitely, and that orders for single or multiple copies can quickly be supplied.

The Cambridge Library Collection brings back to life books of enduring scholarly value (including out-of-copyright works originally issued by other publishers) across a wide range of disciplines in the humanities and social sciences and in science and technology.

College Life

Letters to an Under-Graduate

Thomas Whytehead

CAMBRIDGE
UNIVERSITY PRESS

CAMBRIDGE
UNIVERSITY PRESS

University Printing House, Cambridge, CB2 8BS, United Kingdom

Cambridge University Press is part of the University of Cambridge.
It furthers the University's mission by disseminating knowledge in the pursuit of
education, learning and research at the highest international levels of excellence.

www.cambridge.org
Information on this title: www.cambridge.org/9781108078771

© in this compilation Cambridge University Press 2017

This edition first published 1845
This digitally printed version 2017

ISBN 978-1-108-07877-1 Paperback

COLLEGE LIFE.

COLLEGE LIFE.

LETTERS

TO

AN UNDER-GRADUATE.

BY THE REV.

THOMAS WHYTEHEAD, M.A.

LATE FELLOW OF ST. JOHN'S COLLEGE, CAMBRIDGE; AND CHAPLAIN
TO THE BISHOP OF NEW ZEALAND.

CAMBRIDGE:
JOHN THOMAS WALTERS.
LONDON: JAMES BURNS. OXFORD: J. H. PARKER.
M.DCCC.XLV.

CAMBRIDGE:
JOHN THOMAS WALTERS,
6 King's Parade.

CONTENTS.

———

EDITOR'S PREFACE.

THOMAS WHYTEHEAD was born at Thormanby, in the North Riding of the County of York, on St. Andrew's Day 1815, and died in his twenty-eighth year at Waimate, Bay of Islands, New Zealand, on the Third Sunday in Lent, 19th of March 1843. He was the youngest son of the Rev. Henry Robert Whytehead, B.A., and of Hannah Diana, daughter of the Rev. Thomas Bowman, M.A., Rector of Crayke, in the County of Durham, and Prebendary of Lincoln. From the death of his father, which took place in

his third year, to his removal to Beverley
Grammar School before he had completed
his ninth, he remained with three brothers
and five sisters under the care of his mother
at York; his education meanwhile being
conducted by a valued instructress, who
had charge of the younger members of the
family. At Beverley he continued until the
close of the year 1830, first under the Rev.
G. P. Richards, M.A., Senior Fellow of King's
College, Cambridge, and afterwards under the
Rev. T. S. Warren, M. A. The rest of his
preparation for the University was carried on
by his brother the Rev. Robert Whytehead.
In October 1833, he came into residence as
Pensioner at St. John's College, Cambridge;
and took the degrees of B. A. in 1837, and
M. A. in 1840. During his academical
course he obtained College Prizes for Decla-
mation, Latin Verse, Reading the Lessons
in Chapel, and place in the Examination
Classes; also the University Honours of the

"first" Bell's Scholarship, the Chancellor's
Medal for English Verse (twice), Sir W.
Browne's Medal for Greek and Latin Epi-
grams, and the Hulsean Prize: he was also
second in the first class of the Classical
Tripos, and senior Chancellor's Medallist.

On the 13th of March 1837, he was elected
a Foundation Fellow of his College, and in
the following year he was appointed Classical
Lecturer of Clare Hall. He was ordained
Deacon by the Bishop of Winchester to the
Curacy of Freshwater, in the Isle of Wight,
at Christmas 1839, and Priest at Christmas 1840. In October 1841, he became
Chaplain to the Bishop of New Zealand,
with whom he shortly afterwards set sail,
and reached Sidney in May 1842. Soon
after landing he ruptured a blood-vessel,
owing to which he was detained five months
in New South Wales. At length, on the 22nd
of October, he arrived at New Zealand, where
he lingered in a gradual decline until his

death in the following spring. He was borne
to the grave, at their own request, by the
six students of the Bishop's newly-established
College, of which he was the first Principal,
and he lies buried at the east end of Waimate
Church.

The following work was composed in the
early part of the year 1841, while the author
was Curate of Freshwater. The subject was
one that had been long present to his mind.
He had, as he used to say, much enjoyed
College himself, and he wished to aid others
towards enjoying it also. It was, however,
for some time a matter of perplexity to him
to determine what would be the most suitable
form in which to cast his thoughts. "I
think," he says in a memorandum dated
Feb. 6, 1841, "the Student must be written
in the form of a dialogue. I cannot tell
how else to bring in what I want, and escape
difficulties. The *present form* of College Life
is so unlike the idea." George Herbert's

Country Parson next suggested itself as a model, and on its plan he sketched out several chapters. At length he fixed upon the epistolary form. Still he was not satisfied with what he had written; and with these feelings he laid aside the papers for a time, intending to take up and complete them on some future occasion. The subsequent history of the work will best appear from part of a letter which he wrote to the editor from the Waimate, Bay of Islands, New Zealand, March 14, 1843, five days before his decease. After describing the state of weakness to which he was reduced, "I wish earnestly," he continues, "I could comply with your suggestion and desire of my going on with the 'Letters to a Student,' with some alterations of the plan making it more practical. But while I was in Australia, for those three months when I might have completed it, my papers were in New Zealand, and I knew not in which of my

numerous boxes. Arrived at N. Z. I was
too much troubled with asthma and lethargy
to write. As I recovered from this I took
up the translation of the Evening Hymn
(four verses for service) into Maori rhyming
verse, the first of the kind, of the same metre
and rhythm as the English. Two hundred
and fifty copies have been printed, and sung
in church and school by the natives, and several
of them came and sang it under my window.
They call it 'the new hymn of the sick minister.' Now I found this a harder and longer
task than I had anticipated; and I needed the
assistance of the experienced Missionaries to
correct my use of the particles, in which the
natives are very precise, and in many other
points, in which my very imperfect knowledge
of the language failed me. Bishop Ken's
lines moreover it is very hard for one to com-
press within the same bounds in a rude language. However it is done, and people seem
pleased with it; and it is a comfort to think

one has introduced Bishop Ken's beautiful
Hymn into the Maori's Evening Worship, and
left them this legacy when I could do no more
for them. One thousand more copies were
struck off to-day, for the Southern Congrega-
tions. As I said before, I found this a longer
task than I thought; need of new corrections
kept being discovered; and I found my private
reading much given up, and my thoughts too
much taken up by my work, pleasant as it
was, for one so near the entrance of the
shadowy valley as I am. I assure you I felt
to breathe quite freely when I had signed the
Imprimatur on the last proof copy. Now the
same reason makes me unwilling to undertake
anything else in the way of composition:
moreover I still do not know where the papers
lie, and I wish the boxes to remain unopened,
tinned as they are, to be sent home at my
decease. Will you befriend this parcel of
MS. papers? with full permission to burn
them, or keep them by you, till you have got

your degree, but by no means to meddle with them before; and then, if you are so disposed, make use of them towards the composition of such a volume as you described to me."

It might perhaps seem from this letter, that the Editor had only to choose between destroying the papers or completing the Work. The thought of publishing them as they are does not appear to have occurred to the Author. Still no one can doubt that, had it been proposed to him, his only consideration would have been whether they were sufficiently finished to be of use. On this point there can surely be little question. Besides the very completeness of the papers, though they want much of that fulness and finish which they would have received at the Author's hands, had he been spared to accomplish his design, would have rendered it almost impossible so to engraft upon them a new work as that the original materials should be preserved untouched and distinct. Even in their present state, however, they put forward a view of College Life very different from the one ordinarily taken; but it is the only view which will give unity to the several parts of the system. It was a Religious Idea which our Founders sought to express in the Colleges which they founded; and, if we interpret their Institutions on any other assumption, the result can only be an unmeaning confusion.

T. F. K.

TRINITY COLLEGE, CAMBRIDGE,
May, 1845.

INTRODUCTION.

Οὔ πώ σφιν ἐξίτηλον αἷμα δαιμόνων.

IT is a most true observation, that "Institutions come to nothing when they aban-
don the principles which they embody;" and
we cannot but think of this with some anxiety,
when we consider the nature of the various
changes which have of late years, from within
as well as from without, been suggested with
respect to our present University and College
system; almost all of them advocating the
taking up of new ground, rather than the
recovery, so far as is practicable, of that which

we once occupied. To those who are in the habit of undervaluing or disregarding all such forces as are not reducible to statistical calculation, much of what I shall here say of those time-consecrated influences and associations, with which our ancient Collegiate Institutions are by their very antiquity so richly endowed, will probably appear visionary and fanciful. Let such, however, remember that there are those who believe that it is through the feelings more than the understanding that the Inner Man is to be reached and the soul awoke; that the Imagination is as Divine a part of man as his Reason, and is that which is to be especially cultivated in youth; since, as one deeply says, "Thought without Reverence is barren, perhaps poisonous:" "Wouldst thou plant for Eternity, then plant into the deep infinite faculties of man, his Fantasy and Heart; wouldst thou plant for Year and Day, then plant into his shallow superficial faculties, his Self-love and Arithmetical Understand-

ing."[1]   At all events I shall speak here of
influences, the effects of which I have felt
myself, and traced in those around me; and
my object in these letters will be not to suggest changes, even such as I might think
desirable, for I write mainly to under-graduates, but to take the Collegiate system *as it
is,* and attempt to show how it still exhibits
opportunities for carrying out most advan-
tageously the principles of our statutes.   I
shall try to give the student some insight into
the character and origin of these Foundations, such as may help him to enter into
the spirit of these Institutions and of the
Place, by bringing out, wherever it is still
discernible, the traces of their original rise
out of the Monasteries and Monastic schools:
the spirit for founding them taking its rise
as that for founding Monasteries declined.

I know few greater aids and assistances to

---

[1] Sartor Resartus, p. 233.

the religious principles of a young student
than such associations, fostering as they do a
spirit of Reverence, and converting unmeaning laws and ceremonials into venerable symbols of living Truths. The remembrance of
the great and good, who have trodden before
him the path he is here called to walk, will
animate and invigorate him, and that prayer
uttered by one of old will often arise from
him with reference to them, "O Domine, da
ut non degenerem ab excelsis cogitationibus
filiorum Dei!"

The temptations indeed and dangers of
College have, I am persuaded, been much
exaggerated. I doubt whether there is any
other course of life which presents to the
young beginner so few temptations to ill, and
in which the path to be pursued lies so
straight before him, and the inducements to
right doing are so strong.

Martyrs to study are very rare. Many
more injure their health by neglect of study,

than by excess of it. Many parents, sending a son to College who has delicate health, direct him not to try to read for Honours. This is a great mistake. In the present state of the system of our Universities, where the examination for Honours stands almost in the place which that for Degrees used to occupy, such a one finds himself excluded from the main interests of the place, and with very little provision made for him.

I shall not make any apology for having omitted in these letters those "pro forma" sentences, which usually denote their opening and conclusion. The epistolary form seemed most suitable to my purpose, and for that reason solely I adopted it; and though the letters are written as addressed to an undergraduate, I hope they may not be found void of some thoughts which may be useful even to those of older standing.

THE ORIGIN AND END OF THE COLLEGIATE SYSTEM.

LETTER I.

THE ORIGIN AND END OF THE COLLEGIATE SYSTEM.

THERE are some students who pass through College, much in the same way as the common race of travellers pass through foreign countries: they know and care little about the history of what they see around them, and consequently lose well nigh all the interest and benefit of their residence there, and come away full of misapprehensions, and almost as perfect strangers as when they went. You however, I know, are of a very different temper. You find yourself enrolled a member of a famous fraternity, surrounded by

venerable institutions and ancient laws and
ceremonials, and you wish to know something
of their history, that you may be able to enter
into their spirit and character. Now believe
me, this is the way to enjoy to the full the
time spent at the University. It will thus
become to you something more than a school
where you are sent to get prizes, and your
College more than a boarding-house. You
will come to regard them both with a high
and reverential and affectionate feeling, which
it will be the object of these letters to call
forth, as the home which has adopted you
when you were sent forth from your father's
roof, till you should be of age to make for
yourself a home of your own.

I intend to speak more especially of the
student as a member of his *College*, considering his relation to the *University* little more
than as it bears on and serves to illustrate
this; for it is the Collegiate system, as exhibited in Cambridge and Oxford, which I wish

principally here to open out to you.   I shall
also throughout regard the student as a member of the Foundation of his College; inas-
much as, though he may be receiving nothing
from the Endowment, and so consider himself as under no obligations to the Founder,
the case is indeed far otherwise.   The privilege of residence in College, wherever it is
conceded to others besides the Fellows and
Scholars, is granted under strict condition of
conformity with the laws and regulations of
the Society.   And this provision was made,
in order that, while no member of the University might be excluded from sharing the
benefits and discipline of such a home as the
Colleges afforded, the rules of the Foundation
might at the same time be not in danger of
being relaxed.

Having premised thus much, I will now go
on to give you a slight sketch of the rise and
history of these Institutions, and how they
came to be set up in our Universities; just

enough to help us towards arriving at what Coleridge would have called "the idea" of our Collegiate system, that is, according to his definition, "that conception of it which is given by a knowledge of its ultimate aim." This is the only way in which we can hope to obtain a true view and apprehension of the character of these Foundations, and to enter rightly into the spirit of College life.

The Collegiate Foundations, both in England and the Continent, seem to have taken their rise from those Halls or Claustral schools, as they were called, which the great religious Orders, especially those of the Benedictines and Augustinians, first established in several of the University towns for the reception of the novices of their respective bodies and such others of their members as resorted thither either as teachers or learners. These Monastic Institutions, about the middle of the thirteenth century, gave rise to similar Foundations for the benefit of poor scholars. Of

these, some were merely halls or hostels,
where the students lived together with the
benefit of free board and lodging; provision
being also made for a master and one or
more assistant-graduates, to regulate the discipline and direct the studies of the inmates:
while in others a further endowment was provided for the support of a body of resident
graduates, who, living under a certain rule
laid down in their statutes of a strictly ecclesiastical character, were to devote themselves
to theological and other studies.   In England
however, far more than on the Continent, the
Colleges were the actual successors of the
Monasteries, and partook largely of their
character and constitution.

Judging from what remains of the original
charters, the education of the young was by
no means the *only*, scarcely even the *primary*,
object of our Collegiate Foundations; though
in the reviews made of the statutes under
Queen Elizabeth and her two successors this

object was brought forward with much greater prominence. The charter, for example, given in 1511, for the erection of St. John's College, Cambridge, ordains it to be a perpetual body of persons "in scientiis liberalibus, et sacra theologia *studentium* et *oraturorum.*"[1]

To establish schools from which the Church might be supplied with able defenders and disciplined and well-instructed Priests, — to give opportunity for studious men to lay up stores of learning, especially in theology, the queen and mother of all sciences, — to train them in habits of devotion, self-restraint, frugality, and obedience,[2]— these were plainly leading motives among those which prompted these magnificent Foundations. It has been well expressed elsewhere, "The glory of God, His services, the good of His Church, to be

---

[1] Baker's Preface [in the appendix to Hymers' edition of The Lady Margaret's Funeral Sermon,] p. 27.

[2] Let me refer the reader to an able article in the British Critic, No. 54, on Magdalen. Coll. Stat. on this subject.

sought by the self-dedication of zealous men to the study of His word, and of all the subsidiary means of understanding it."[1]

They are now the sole-surviving representatives in the English Church of that Monastic element which the Colleges and the Capitular bodies once exhibited in common, as having for their object the maintenance of a class of men, mainly of the Clergy, whose duties should not connect them with active and public life, but rather withdraw them from out of the influence of the age they lived in. These were intended to give a *permanence* and *stability* to the character of the Institutions in the midst of which they were placed. Standing out of the current of the world and of the times, their duty was to prevent their fellows and countrymen from being carried down by it, who might else imagine they were standing still, only because every thing

---

[1] Quart. Rev. No. 131, June 1840 [p. 165].

around them was being drifted along with them. Such was the firm and energetic Laud, when, at forty years old, he quitted Oxford, to become, as one has called him, "the second founder" of the English Church.

The Past is here to have always, as it were, its *living representatives,* who may be able to confute all false claims to novelty which the Present may put forward, and save the world from being obliged to recover lost truths again and again by the costly method of experiment. It has been truly said that "whatever withdraws us from the power of our senses, whatever makes the past, the distant, or the future predominate over the present, advances us in the scale of rational beings:" and this is the object of the Collegiate system as placed in the midst of our Universities; and the absence of this system is the key to the essential difference between them and the Universities of Scotland and the Continent. The principle of independence on external influences, provided by the presence of these bodies, is there wanting; they generally are controlled by, instead of controlling, the spirit of the times; they are the representatives of the national temper, not its directors. Accordingly, as one has said of the English Collegiate bodies, "it is *their place* to be old-fashioned;" or rather the fine description which Schiller has given us of what he calls the perfect "artist" will, with some few alterations, best represent to you the character which the statutes of our Colleges wish to perpetuate in the members of their Foundations. "The artist," says he, "it is true, is the son of his age; but pity for him if he is its pupil, or even its favourite! Let some beneficent divinity snatch him, when a suckling, from the breast of his mother, and nurse him with the milk of a better time, that he may ripen to his full stature beneath a distant Grecian sky: and having grown to manhood, let him return a foreign shape into his

c

century; not however to delight it by his presence, but dreadful, like the son of Agamemnon, to purify it. The *matter* of his works he will take from the present, but their *form* he will derive from a nobler time; nay, from beyond all time, from the absolute unchanging unity of his own nature."

Such being the spirit of these Foundations and the character they are designed to form, the student, if he be of the class of those who come to College to train themselves for active life, not with a view of fixed residence, regards the three years he spends there, as bearing a likeness to the Vigil which the knights of old used to keep in Church just before they received their sword of Knighthood, and were sent forth to do service in the world.[1]   He therefore seeks retirement as far as possible,

---

[1] Let me here suggest to my reader to trace out some of the many elements which connect that wonderful period in the world's history, the age of chivalry, of "cnighthade," (the term by which our Anglo-Saxon forefathers distinguished the

listens to catch as much as he may of the still
and distant voice of the Past, knowing that to
him it will soon be drowned in the noise and
bustle of the Present, in order that hereafter
from them both he may be able to form a wise
and "serene prescience of the Future."   He
is here like young Achilles in the cave of the
Centaur, and regards without a smile, nay
with something of an affectionate reverence,
the very eccentricities and peculiarities which
belong to the quaint old-fashioned minds
under whose guardianship he is placed.   And
even in the absence of minds of this antique
cast among the heads of his College,—should
he be so unfortunate as to fall among a body
of residents who represent only the spirit of the
world about them, and therefore fail of one of
the great purposes for which they were placed
here, namely to form a visible link between

---

period between childhood and manhood,) with the time of
youth in ourselves. See "that right noble and joyous book"
the "Broadstone of Honour."

the life of past ages and the present,—still the
College will have habitually in his mind such
a distinct personality, independent of its existing members, that its voice will be to him
what that of the Church has been to many a
gentle soul in the English, or Greek, or Latin
branches of it in an age of degenerate faith
or practice. He will appeal from the degenerate living representative to the undying
original which it represents, and so will acquire by degrees the important power and
habit of seeing the *ideal* in the *actual,* of re-
cognizing and paying homage to it even under
its present imperfect development. Nor is it
to imaginative and susceptible minds alone
that the voice of the spirit of antiquity is thus
audible, breathing throughout the whole fabric
of our Collegiate Institutions. He that will
listen may hear it. The reverence paid to
founders, reaching with pious duty to their
sepulchres and their kindred, the commemora-
tions of benefactors, the adherence to ancient

costume and ceremonials are all *retrospective* in their character, and are peculiarly suited to act upon and affect a youthful mind, as being in strong contrast with its own naturally *prospective* disposition, just as

> " Then, Twilight is preferred to Dawn,
> And Autumn to the Spring."

But of the character of the true College student, as taking its form from the mould in which these Institutions are designed to cast it, I will speak more at large in my next letter.

COLLEGE DISCIPLINE.

LETTER II.

THE very first step towards entering into the true spirit of college life is to learn to view yourself here as in a state of discipline and pupilage; and, what is more, to rejoice that it should be so. Of this be sure, that the submission of your own will and judgment to the system of the place is of itself a far more valuable exercise than could at all be compensated for by any self-devised improvement on the course you find marked out for you. Beautiful, and most worthy of remembrance, are those words of the Wise Man, "the very true beginning of wisdom is the desire of discipline; and the care of discipline is love; and love is the keeping of her laws." This is an essential part of the College student's character, to regard superiors, and especially seniors, with reverence and honour, and to pay a glad and graceful obedience to discipline and law.

Perhaps there is nothing which so much tends to make the years spent at College so happy a part of a student's life as they generally are, as the light-hearted feeling of irresponsibility arising from our having the way of duty here clearly marked out, (so that we are freed from the anxiety of choosing it for ourselves, and have only to follow it,) and the singleness and simplicity of purpose, which a docile submission to this guidance creates. There is indeed, as an able writer has expressed it, "a painfulness in the very sense of entire responsibility, a bitterness in the full cup of freedom from control, which those who drink most freely of it are the first to taste. A thoughtful mind will scarcely look on any condition as

more deserving of pity than his who enters
upon life

" Lord of himself, that heritage of woe :"

and in the full liberty of the mind before it
is fixed by sympathy in its choice, there is an
oppression from which the most vigorous understanding hastens the soonest to escape."[1]

It is with reference to this that Dr. John-
son writes to his friend.Baretti: "I do not
wonder that where the monastic life is permitted, every order finds votaries, and every
monastery inhabitants. Men will submit to
any rule by which they may be exempted from
the tyranny of caprice and of chance. They
are glad to supply by external authority their
own want of constancy and resolution, and
court the government of others, when long
experience has convinced them of their own
inability to form themselves."   Now this

---

[1] British Critic, No. 49, p. 147.

craving of our nature, if abused, leads to
the worst form of jesuitical self-enslavement,
destroying all true moral obedience; but put
under due limits it is a most religious principle, and as such was worthily commended in
the dying words of that wise and holy man
Dr. Hammond, who, when he was asked by a
friend what special thing he would recommend
for one's whole life, briefly replied, *" uniform
obedience ;"* by which he meant, as his biographer, Dr. Fell, tells us, that the happiest state
of life was one which imposed on us the condition of *obeying* rather than *directing;* the lot
of *not having to choose for one's self,* but having
our path of duty marked out for us.   In just
such a state of life is the student placed at
College; and the spirit which pervades the
whole of Wordsworth's fine Ode to Duty
exactly represents the tone of feeling which
ought to be habitual to his mind.

[This truth comes more especially home to

such students as are destined hereafter for
Holy Orders.] The importance of having the
end clear before one, " quo tendis et in quod
dirigis arcum," of feeling oneself under restraint, not in "unchartered freedom," is a
blessing and a safeguard beyond price during
one's College life. The very prospect of one's
Ordination Vow is a great help, a sacrament
at times. "All vows lessen the number of
indifferent actions to the person bound
thereby:" and so *in its degree* the very
prospect of this vow. Ἐγὼ μὲν γὰρ οἶμαι,
says Demosthenes, (κ. Ἀνδροτ.) δεῖν τὸν εἰς
ἱερὰ εἰσιόντα, καὶ χερνίβων καὶ κανῶν ἁψόμενον,
καὶ τῆς πρὸς τοὺς Θεοὺς ἐπιμελείας προστάτην
ἐσόμενον, οὐχὶ προειρημένον ἡμερῶν ἀριθμὸν
ἁγνεύειν, ἀλλὰ τὸν βίον ὅλον ἡγνευκέναι τοιού-
των ἐπιτηδευμάτων οἷα τούτῳ βεβίωται. I shall
make no excuse for having given you so long
a quotation, as if you have not observed or
read it before, it is a passage well worthy of

being known to you, and, I might say, com-
mitted to memory.[1]

Moreover, the very dress which the student
wears as a member of the University reminds him, should he ever be in danger of
forgetting it, that he is not his own master,
—that he is here subject to a system of discipline and laws. It is in this like that
fringe and riband of blue which every
Israelite was commanded to wear on the
border of his garment, "that they might
look on it, and remember all the commandments of the Lord, and do them; and that
they might seek not after their own heart
and their own eyes, but remember and do
all His commandments, and be holy unto
their God." And from this consideration too
the student, if he ever come to be in Holy
Orders, thinks it of importance to observe
any badge of dress yet remaining which may

---

[1] The above passage is taken from a letter to a friend. [Ed.]

outwardly mark his clerical character, and thus serve as a kind of livery to remind himself, as well as others, that he is God's servant, set apart to do His work. To an ecclesiastic residing in College all such remembrances are especially desirable, lest in the absence of the usual clerical functions he come at any time to forget his office. Nor does what I have just said about dress apply to ecclesiastics alone. Our old College statutes wisely ordained that a grave and sober habit, (a term singularly expressive,) and one such as may become priests to wear, should be worn not by them only, but by *all* other members of the University:—consistently with the unworldly light in which they are here uniformly regarded, as the temporary lay members of an ecclesiastical order; the candidates for a degree conferred in the Name of the Ever-blessed Trinity. .

The allegiance and subordination of which I have been speaking is at present required to a *traditionary*, rather than a *written* code of laws. Many of the specific regulations prescribed in the original bodies of Statutes having, in most of the Colleges, been gradually displaced and become obsolete, through the silent change of manners and perhaps too ready concession to external influences, the authoritative practice and the system of Academic discipline now enforced embodies to a great extent the *spirit* of the more ancient written laws; but the study of these latter is still most necessary to the student, even were it only to understand rightly our existing usages and regulations.

I will make no further remark on the present system of practice and discipline, but only express my regret that the regulation common to most of our old Foundations, which enjoins that the whole body of Statutes should be read aloud in the hearing of all the residents twice or thrice a year, is so generally disused. It was thus provided by

the Founders that all scholars and fellows
should be fully aware beforehand what those
Statutes are which they take oath to observe;[1]
and in very few cases could a person become
a member of these Foundations without having first resided for some time as a sort of
probationer. In this respect it is interesting
to trace the resemblance between the constitution of the Monastic and that of the Collegiate bodies.

---

[1] With reference to this much-embarrassed subject of Collegiate Oaths, I would observe here, that, as every oath is
taken and considered binding "in sensu Imponentis," the
main question to be resolved is, who is in this case the
"Imponens?" Certainly not the Founder *alone*, for the
present statutes are in the elder Foundations the work of
Archbishop Whitgift and others, and are very different from
the originals. In the last of Bishop Sanderson's admirable
Lectures "De Juramenti Obligatione" is a remark which bears
strongly on the present state of our statutes: "Relaxation by
a Party is of force, *as far as that Party is concerned*, but is
not of force to the prejudice of a Third Person." Now is
not the deceased Founder in the present instance exactly such
a third person? I cordially agree with Dean Peacock that
the sooner the *wording* of our University oaths is altered, the
better.

D

The famous threefold vow which met the Novice at his first asking for admission into any of the great Monastic Orders was, as you know, that of perpetual Poverty, Obedience, and Chastity. This weighty engagement he was not allowed to take upon himself hastily or all at once; indeed by the Rules of several of the Oriental Monasteries it was forbidden that any one should be admitted until he was of such age as to have arrived at the full honours of a beard. In the Rule of the Order of St. Benedict, as reformed by Gregory IX. and Innocent IV., the law respecting the admission of Novices was framed very wisely in this respect. After one or more years of trial had passed, the Rule under which he was about to enrol himself being read aloud to him three times during each year of his noviciate, the candidate for admission was finally addressed in these words, "Behold the Rule under which thou desirest to enlist thyself. If thou be able to keep it, enter; if not, thou

art free to depart." The young Benedictine
hereupon having made solemn vow by God's
help to obey, and never renounce it, laid his
written declaration to this effect on the Altar
of the Chapel; and then, solemn prayer being
offered up for him and with him by the assem-
bled Brethren of the Order, and the Gloria
Patri having been sung by all together, the
young Monk was invested with the dress of
his Order, and the blessing being given, all
retired to their cells. Such was the form of
admission into the most deservedly celebrated
of the old Monastic Orders, and that required
by the others very much resembled it. Now
this famous threefold vow is represented in the
statutes of most of the older Foundations in
the two Universities by the principle, which
pervades them all, of enjoining in their members plainness of living, (having, as far as may
be, all things in common,) strictness of discipline, and the maintenance of the Celibate.
Moreover, as I said before, we have also in

effect a period of noviciate, in the provision
which is made [in] our system for acquainting
our members with the Statutes to which they
bind themselves: while in one essential point
the later Foundations excel in wisdom the
more ancient, that whereas the vow of the
Monk was irrevocable, that of the member
of a Collegiate body may be revoked at
pleasure.

The following lines were written by Ambrose Bonwicke, who died at St. John's College, Cambridge, in the twenty-third year of
his age, A.D. 1714, in his copy of Dr. Lake's
Officium Eucharisticum, and contain a *Rule*
for the formation of Christian character which
can scarcely be surpassed.   I cannot find who
was the author of them, or whether they were
written by himself.

> Fide Deo, dic sæpe preces, peccare caveto,
> Sis humilis, pacem dilige, magna fuge.
> Multa audi, dic pauca, tace abdita, scito minori
> Parcere, majori cedere, ferre parem.
> Propria fac, persolve fidem, sis æquus egenis,
> Parta tuere, pati disce, memento mori.

I cannot more usefully conclude this letter, on the spirit of submission to Collegiate discipline, than by an extract, though somewhat long, from a sermon on the subject of "The Student's Walk," which I am glad to take this opportunity of commending to your notice :—

"There is no disposition in our day to deny, or even to yield reluctant obedience to the authority of Academic discipline and the rules of Academic propriety, when adequately understood or explained. Be it permitted us, however, to say, that perhaps it is not by any of us adequately either understood or explained. We are too much accustomed to take our standard from the world's usages from which we are for a while come out, and from which we are come out for the express purpose of acquiring some familiarity with a higher, a graver, more serious, more religious standard, by which we may help to regulate and reform, when we go back

again, that which the world has adopted,
and which is more subject to fluctuation and
deterioration than ours. We ought therefore
carefully to be on our guard against thinking
a thing is right here, because it is the custom of general society: much more ought we
to beware of unsettling or contemning the
rules and customs of our Institutions here,
which were made with a view to stand amidst
the fleeting changes of worldly practice, on
the comfortable but treacherous excuse that
such rules are impracticable and such customs
are gone by." [1]

---

[1] The Student's Walk. [A Sermon by Archdeacon
T. Thorp.] p. 12.

COLLEGE ROOMS.

LETTER III.

COLLEGE ROOMS.

THE student loves no place out of holy ground so well as his rooms: here is his home, his laboratory, his monastic cell. All gay and expensive furniture he feels would be quite out of place here, and would rather choose to imitate the simple inventory of the prophet's chamber at Shunem. The only ornaments he allows, beside his books, are perhaps two or three pictures, selected as the companions of his room with the same heedful choice which he uses in the forming of

his acquaintance or the gathering of his
library.

> There hung upon the walls
> Whereon his eyes would rest at intervals
> A few choice pictures: here on reverent knee
> Was offering of her flowers Saint Amelie:
> And there an infant Christ, in desert wild,
> Gave high commission to the marvellous child
> That knelt before Him, Mary looking on;
> While next unto an angel-faced Saint John
> The martyr-king with calm complaining eye
> Looked forth from out a frame of ebony.

There are few sets of rooms in any of the
older Colleges which have not some traditionary connexion with the names of one or other
of the famous sons of the family of which he
is now enrolled a member.   Indeed the whole
ground of our two Universities is consecrated
to the memory of their illustrious men.   It is
quick with stirring associations and recollec-
tions: and those who in their estimate of the
value of a College education allow little for
the force of this " Religio loci " in the forming
of a high tone of character, lose sight of one

of the most powerful instruments for this end
which our Universities possess. The student
looks on the venerable building in which his
dwelling is placed with a sort of family pride,
as the home that has already sent out into the
world so many noble and generous sons, yea
and learned and holy sons too, and from
which he himself must soon in his turn go
forth, bearing with him in his measure the
responsibility of sustaining the ancient honour
of the fraternity. Nor does he forget those
gentle spirits who, by nature unfitted to en-
counter the throng and turmoil of public life,
have from time to time found a shelter within
these walls, and the fruits of whose pious and
laborious retirement posterity is even now
inheriting. "I have sought for rest every-
where," said Thomas à Kempis towards the
close of his life, "but I have found it nowhere
except in a little corner with a little book:"
and so too might Grabe have said at Oxford,
and Thomas Baker at Cambridge, and many

others of like honoured name. If his College
has been originally a Monastic Foundation
he will think with pleasure of those gentle
spirits who realized, or thought they realized,
here those words of St. Bernard inscribed on
the walls of many of the Cistertian Houses,
"Bonum est nos hic esse, quia homo vivit
purius, cadit rarius, surgit velocius, incedit
cautius, quiescit securius, moritur felicius,
purgatur citius, præmiatur copiosius."

> "Here man more purely lives, less oft doth fall,
> More promptly rises, walks with stricter heed,
> More safely rests, dies happier, is freed
> Earlier from cleansing fires, and gains withal
> A brighter crown."[1]

Of such was our countryman Gyraldus
Cambrensis, whose lines on his cell at
St. Alban's are not without a touching and
simple beauty :—

> "Claustrum
> Martyris Albani sit tibi tuta quies.
> Hic locus ætatis nostræ primordia novit,
> Annos felices, lætitiæque dies."

---

[1] Wordsworth's [Ecclesiastical Sonnets.]

Of such too was, in later times, that holy
youth Ambrose Bonwicke, whose life exhibits
the most perfect pattern of a Christian student which our times have seen.

There is something very touching in the
words in which good Bishop Hall, at the end
of his long and troublous life, speaks of the
six or seven years of diligent study he passed
in Cambridge at Emmanuel College, after
having been elected a Fellow of that Society,
" which," says he, " I spent with such con-
tentment as the rest of my life has in vain
striven to yield."   I should be passing over
too a most beautiful, as well as famous, example of the affectionate feelings with which
men of honoured name have looked back on a
well-spent College life, were I to omit notice
of that most touching "Farewell" to his friends,
and to the places with which he had been
connected, which Bishop Ridley wrote from
his prison at Oxford.   In that affecting letter
(which, though well known, you may not have

by you to refer to), after making mention of
Cambridge, his " loving mother and tender
nurse," saying, " If I should not acknowledge
thy manifold benefits, yea if I should not for
thy benefits, at the least, love thee again, truly
I were to be counted ingrate and unkind." He
goes on to write, " Farewell, Pembroke Hall,
of late mine own College, my cure, and my
charge. In thy orchard (the walls, butts, and
trees, if they could speak, would bear me witness,) I learned without book almost all Paul's
Epistles: yea and, I ween, all the Canonical
Epistles, save only the Apocalypse. Of which
study, though in time a great part did depart
from me, yet the sweet smell thereof I trust
I shall carry with me into heaven: for the
profit thereof I think I have felt in all my
lifetime ever after."

The Collegiate system, as carried out in the
two Universities, is beautifully adapted to the
formation of a character solid and retiring, and
at the same time not that of a recluse. With

opportunities for undisturbed retirement and
lonely study is combined the perpetually recurring idea of common interests and duties,
and close brotherly connexion with the Society
to which the student belongs: his thoughts and
feelings are thus constantly directed towards
an object external to himself, in whose honour
and welfare he is intimately concerned, and
his natural feelings of ardour and affection
find a locality and centre around which they
may gather in the *person* of his College.

It is a very beautiful description which
Thomas à Kempis gives of the manner of
daily life of himself and his fellow students
at the College at Daventer, one of the schools
belonging to the " Society of Regular Canons,"
of which Florentius, Vicar of the principal
Church, was the head: and as those schools
seem to have borne a greater resemblance
than any other middle-age Institutions of
which we read to our later Collegiate Foundations, it may not be profitless to introduce

it here. " Much was I delighted with the devout conversation, the irreproachable manners, and the humility of my brethren. I had never seen such piety or charity. Taking no concern in what passed beyond their walls, they remained at home, employed in prayer and study, or in copying useful books, and sanctifying this occupation by short but frequent ejaculations of devotion. In the morning they went to church, and dedicated the first fruits of their hearts to God. They appeared to have but one mind and one soul. Their dress was homely; their diet was spare; their obedience to their superiors without reserve."

The little society of scholars thus described was placed in the house of a respectable matron in the town, who furnished them gratuitously with their board and lodging.[1]

---

[1] Butler's Preface [to the " Imitatio Christi," p. ii.]

The rules of the several Foundations, which enjoin daily attendance at Chapel and Hall and on other public duties, wisely forbid hereby anything like an eremitical life, and so provide as far as may be against most of the dangers incident to solitary habits; [and among these, against the formation of] an ungentle, self-sufficient temper, which is so opposite to that of the Christian scholar, the "puer Christi," as Erasmus calls him.

In cases of temptation, "nemo videt" is a dangerous suggestion. Connected with this there is the Wise Man's warning concerning lonely living, "Woe to him that is alone when he falleth, for he hath not another to help him up." Indeed the extreme danger of an utterly solitary life was always acknowledged, even in those times which were most disposed to exalt it. The 41st Canon of the Council of Trullo forbad any one to undertake an eremitical life, unless after

E

having lived three years *within* a monastery
apart, and one year on trial *out* of its wall;
and in Grimlaïc's[1] Rule for Anchorites, composed
in the ninth century, their cells were
ordered to be near some abbey church, manifestly
as a check on the evils peculiar to a
lonely life. That modified form however of the
cenobitic system which our Colleges present to
the student, seems to realize as far as anything
can, to those who are willing to carry it out,
that happy blending of activity with quietness
which St. Gregory of Nazianzum commends
in his eulogy of St. Athanasius: οὕτω γὰρ
ἀμφότερα συνηρμόσατο, καὶ εἰς ἓν ἤγαγε, καὶ
πρᾶξιν ἡσυχίον καὶ ἡσυχίαν ἔμπρακτον, ὥςτε
πεῖσαι τὸ μονάζειν ἐν τῇ εὐσταθείᾳ τοῦ τρόπου
μᾶλλον ἢ τῇ τοῦ σώματος ἀναχωρήσει χαρακ-
τηρίζεσθαι.[2] "So did he harmonize and blend

---

[1] See Fleury, Hist. Eccles. b. liv. c. 21. [Ed.]
[2] S. Greg. Naz. de Laud. S. Athan. Mag. Orat. xxi.
Opera v. tom. i. pp. 384, 5. Col. Agripp. 1691.

into one both activity in quietness and quietness in activity,[1] that he made the character of the solitary appear to be marked less by bodily loneliness than by spiritual evenness and equability." " We must ever strive after a quiet mind." "Preparation of the heart is the unlearning the prejudices of evil converse. It is the smoothing the waxen tablet before attempting to write on it. Now solitude is of the greatest use for this purpose. Quiet is the first step in our sanctification."[2]

It will be not out of place to notice to you here what a beautiful training is provided in these Institutions for the rearing up of the mind to such a spirit and temper as befits a son of the Catholic Church. Its Unity is shadowed out to the student in the whole

---

[1] Or, " so quiet was he and yet so active, so active and withal so quiet, and these two were in him so blended into harmonious union, &c."

[2] [From a letter of St. Basil to St. Gregory, translated in] " The Church of the Fathers," pp. 132, 133.

system around him, where the individual
member is taught to view himself as in a
state of discipline, bound obediently to main-
tain the order and subserve the interests of
the Body, whose collective greatness and
whose Unity are typified to him in the comparative splendour of the Common Worship
and the Common Table. As has been eloquently observed by a writer on this subject,
speaking of the lesson of dedication to one
common cause which we read in the contrast
between private and public Collegiate buildings, especially those of the earlier Foundations, "What is the moral of the humble
though sufficient chamber of the solitary
student,—the solemn grandeur of the cloister,
the hall, the chapel,—bringing low, even
to nothing, all his individual and personal
importance, while elevating the soul by un-
selfish devotion to the Brotherhood, the
miniature Church which has adopted him?
He must not only do the work of his foun-

dation, but he must do it in the spirit of his foundation; and this we are assured is every day more felt at the Universities."[1] I know that what I have been writing to you applies mainly, and may seem to apply exclusively, to those graduate members of our Collegiate bodies, who have here taken up their residence; and you may think it has little reference to such as enter our Colleges merely for the sake of the education they can obtain there, and are independent of the benefit of the Foundation. But in truth, not to mention the provision made in the statutes, expressly guarding [against] the relaxation of discipline in case of independent members, unless these seek to enter into the spirit of the system around them, they may gain perhaps the knowledge, but certainly not the *education*, which our Collegiate bodies are intended to give. To do this you must seek

---

[1] [Quarterly Review, No. 131, p. 176.]

to imbibe the ἦθος[1] of our Institutions, which, as I have attempted to show, is essentially Monastic and Mediæval. Without such a submission of your mind to their form and spirit, you will never revisit your old College rooms in after life with that feeling of affection which you would entertain, were they associated in your mind not only with the acquisition of knowledge, and perhaps successful competition for University Honours, but with the remembrance of having here made early and happy trial of that truth, which after his public and brilliant career Sir Henry Wotton said that he had at last learned,

"Animas fieri sapientiores quiescendo."

Till your habits as a student are known, and your character established among your

---

[1] In the MS. the word ἦθος is erased, but no other has been substituted. [Ed.]

acquaintance, it will be needful to close your outer door during your hours of study, to prevent interruptions. Be what the monkish writers call "a close keeper of your cell," else time will [slip] away, without your knowing how it goes, by these perpetual inroads.

There is a story told by a monkish writer,[1] something to our purpose, of a young man who was marvelling to an elder how it was that he never discovered any idle thoughts in his heart. "I will tell you how it is," said he; "you sit with all the doorways of your heart open, and whatever chooses passes in and out; but if you shut the door, and forbid idle thoughts coming in, you will see them then in plenty standing outside, battering for entrance." So will you the thieves which steal your time. One of [these writers] has a beautiful passage on this subject in an old devotional book. "Silence and keeping of

---

[1] Thesaur. Ascet. Opusc. ix. p. 235.

thy *cell* are good for the peace of the soul.
Be thou like the prudent bee that, after it
has gathered honey from thy flowers, flies
gladly back and hides it in the cell of its
hive, that it may live on it in secret all the
winter, and not by wandering about waste
the sweetness of what it has gathered. For
precious ointments kept close in a box have
a keener fragrance, but when left open and
unclosed soon lose their odour."

COLLEGE CHAPEL.

LETTER IV.

COLLEGE CHAPEL.

WHEN our ancestors began to build a
College, the chapel was generally the
first part of the edifice which they under-
took, and having finished this, they added the
rest of the building on to it. This, to take
one example from many, was the manner in
which the executors of the Lady Margaret
proceeded to erect her College of St. John's
at Cambridge, and it may serve as a faithful
type of the light in which they regarded the
connexion between the daily worship and the
object of their Collegiate Foundation.

Doubtless indeed in the minds of such of

our Founders as lived during the times of the
Romish supremacy in England, the maintenance of a body of men, who should consider
intercessory prayer, both for the dead and
living, as at least one of the objects for which
they were set apart, held a prominent place;
and the provision which they made for the
chaunting of masses in Chapel for their souls
by those who were receiving their bounty, has
awakened in many a heart the feeling expressed in those simple and affectionate lines
of Baker to his Founder's Picture,—

> " To thee I dare appeal, if thou dost know,
> Or now concern'st thyself with things below,
> Oft had I sent my fervent vows to Heaven,
> Were this the time, or ought were now forgiven."

But there were other causes besides this,
which led them to connect the daily services
in the Chapel so closely with those seminaries
of learning. It was not only that they might
form, as it were, the Family prayer of the
Society, though this they are; it was rather as

a perpetual provision that the Cloister should be felt to join on to the Temple, to be a part of the holy edifice; that the Colleges should be so many Porches of the Church. This view is moreover fully borne out by our Elizabethan Statutes. The whole character of these Foundations is Ecclesiastical, and the Chapel is the type of this character; the secular studies of the place are, as it were, brought hither every day to be blessed and consecrated, so that they may receive a religious impress. For every student received within the walls of the College being regarded as a son of the Church, all his studies are required to wait as handmaids on that Queen-Mother of all Learning — Theology: and this being, as Bishop Taylor has expressed it, " rather a divine life than a divine knowledge," the foundations of the course marked out for him are well and wisely laid in daily prayer and frequent Eucharist.

With respect to this latter provision, you

will find an interesting passage in the life of
that pattern of a Christian student, Ambrose
Bonwicke, where it is said, that being excluded,
as a non-juror, from a scholarship at Oxford,
and subsequently having entered at St. John's
College, Cambridge, his greatest happiness
there, and what he valued above the honours
and profits he had lost, was the frequent re-
turns of the Holy Eucharist, which at that
time he could not have enjoyed at any other
House (Christchurch excepted) in either of the
Universities.

That attendance on the Holy Offices and
instruction in God's Word and the Principles of the Christian Faith should be looked
on as belonging only to the education of a
minister, and not of every member of the
Church, was a notion which the framers of our
Statutes never contemplated.   As a child of
the Church, the student finds himself regarded
as already enrolled among a " Royal Priest-
hood," and, consistently with this view of his

Christian calling, he is called on in his turn
to assist in that part of the daily service, the
reading of the Lessons, in which lay-members
have from very early times been permitted to
officiate. If you view this rightly, you will, I
am sure, look on it as an honourable office,
and one not to be slurred hastily over. In
olden times we know it was so regarded; when
the Emperor Sigismond thought it even an
accession to his high dignity to be allowed
to read the Lessons at the Sessions of the
Council of Constance.

I know it has appeared to many, who
have not rightly and devoutly tried it, that
there must be something cold and formal
in the constant repetition of the same words
of Prayer. But I have the testimony of
the best and holiest Sons of Our Church,
both laymen and divines, on my side, when I
assure you, that if you seek to join solemnly
and earnestly in that daily Ritual, so far from
finding your increased familiarity with its

words a *hindrance* to your devotion, this will
be the greatest help to it. For having to take
no thought of the *language*, but only of the
matter and object of your prayers, you will be
able to give yourself up more entirely to the
One Idea, which ought then to possess your
soul,—that of Him to whom you are speaking;
your desires will come to flow naturally and
undisturbedly in the channels here provided
for them; and the sense of your different
wants will soon habitually arise to your mind
in that form and sequence which the expres-
sion of them in our Liturgy suggests.   It
were almost endless to quote authorities here.
The private memoirs of the Times of King
Charles the Martyr, who himself never missed
attending the daily service, would alone supply
me with a host of witnesses to the truth of
what I have said, from Clarendon, in his lowly
retreat at Guernsey, to Hammond at West-
wood.   But there is one so touching a con-
firmation of this feeling, occurring in Walton's

Memoir of George Herbert, that I cannot refrain from instancing it. He was lying on what proved to be his death-bed, when one Mr. Duncan came to visit him on an errand from a distant friend, and, after some discourse together, "Sir, I see," said he, "by your habit that you are a Priest, and I desire you to pray with me," which being granted, Mr. Duncan asked him, "What prayers?" to which Mr. Herbert's answer was, "O Sir, the prayers of my mother the Church of England; no other prayers are equal to them." So far had been the daily use of the Liturgy, which he constantly observed in his church, from losing any part of its preciousness to him through that repetition.

Let me above all things exhort you to be an early riser, so that the first sounds of the Chapel bell shall find you well nigh prepared to leave your room, that you may be in good time to join with an unruffled spirit in the morning service.

F

Among the many great advantages which
you will derive from the early hour at which
it is usually celebrated, is this very important
one, that it requires the observance of a regular and early hour for going to bed at night;
and so supplies the greatest and most dangerous want which an under-graduate feels on
first coming to College, the absence of the
restraint of Family hours.

It was always to me a solemn and stirring
sight, on some Saint's day morning in the
winter season, more especially that of All
Saints, when the final gathering together of
pure souls is especially brought to mind, to
see the white surplices flitting through the
gloom across the Courts, as the bell ceased to
toll, and disappearing one by one as they
passed into Chapel, their place of assembling;
while the lights within, casting a dim lustre
through the windows, seemed to be, as it were,
a type of the Church of Christ in the midst of
this dark world.

I know that some have complained of the hour of evening Prayers, as it is fixed at most of the Colleges, as interrupting their studies or breaking in on their seasons of recreation. But surely the very necessity, thus perpetually recurring, of having to quit at the call of the Chapel bell some absorbing pursuit or interesting conversation is itself a piece of mental and religious discipline of the greatest possible value.

It is a true and deep view of this, which is given in the following lines from a sonnet on the subject of College Chapel,[1]—

"Best loved, when most thy call did interfere
   With schemes of toil or pleasure, that deceive
   And cheat young hearts; for then thou mad'st me feel
   The Holy Church more nigh, a thing to fear."

A daily attendance at Chapel moreover, morning and evening, gives to a devout mind such an intimate acquaintance with the Psalms,

---

[1] Faber's Poems, p. 103.

unfolding their hidden Christian meanings,
acquainting us with, and teaching how to use,
that divine book which has formed part of
the Church's Ritual for now three thousand
years, as cannot fail to have a great influence
on its tone and temper. As Bishop Horne
has beautifully observed, "the evil spirit is still
dispossessed by the harp of the son of Jesse."
And the wonderful way in which our Blessed
Lord took to Himself the language of this
Book, even so as to breathe out His soul with
part of the thirty-first Psalm on His lips,
justly makes it a privilege of no little value to
be trained up in a daily intimacy with the
Psalter, as our manual of devotion,—a treasure
house of theology, to which the four blessed
Gospels, also daily read in Chapel, are the key
which unlocks it. While however you seek
to make full use of these Public Services, let
me caution you against ever allowing them to
supersede the private devotions of your closet.
This they were never intended to do, and the

absence of these they never can supply. Each soul has individual needs of its own, besetting sins to confess, temptations to pray against, thanksgivings to offer, for which it needs to be alone with God.

In the practice of this duty I would suggest to you, what may assist in bringing your mind into a temper of solemn reverence, to set apart some particular place in your chamber for the purpose of devotion, as in a manner consecrated unto God. "For having a spot thus sacred in your own room," it would in some measure, as Law has observed, "resemble a chapel or House of God, and your own apartment would raise in your mind such sentiments as you have when you stand near an altar." You might hope, each time you returned, to meet in that place with those holy thoughts which possessed you at your last being there.

I cannot refrain from giving you here the very beautiful evening collect which in the

Statutes of several of our Colleges is ordered
to be used by each of the young students just
before going to bed, "devoutly commending
on their knees themselves and their whole
College to God in this short prayer."

"O Rex Gloriose, qui inter sanctos et
electos Tuos semper es laudabilis et tamen
ineffabilis, Tu in nobis es, Domine, et Nomen
Tuum invocatum est super nos; ne derelinquas
nos, Deus noster, sed in die judicii nos collo-
care digneris inter sanctos et electos Tuos,
Rex benedicte.   Salva nos, Domine, vigilantes,
custodi nos dormientes, ut vigilemus cum
Christo, et requiescamus in pace."

THE HALL.

LETTER V.

THE HALL.

HAVING left the Chapel, let me now act as your mystagogue to the College Hall; and I must ask you to look at it with the eyes of a member of the Foundation, not merely a student at the University. In theory most assuredly, whatever they did in practice, our ancestors realized far more than we do now the great Truth, that no action in a Christian's life can be called "common or unclean;" that the very service of his body, as that of a redeemed man, has been ennobled by the taking of the manhood into God; so that whatsoever we do, even to our

eating and drinking, we can do all to the
glory of God. It was this feeling which
doubtless led to representations of the Last
Supper being so often chosen as appropriate
pictures for the refectories of religious houses:
such as that famous painting of Titiano in the
Escurial, where, questionless, many an inmate
besides "the mild Jeronymite" of Wordsworth's most beautiful Poem, have eaten
their daily bread with a more religious and
devout spirit for gazing on "that solemn
company."

Now the portraits of the Founders and
Benefactors and great and reverend men who
have aforetime belonged to our Body, hung
up in our College Halls, do, though in a
lower degree, exhibit this same principle; as
constantly presenting to us, even in the times
of our relaxation, the images of that great
cloud of witnesses who compass us about;—
some with their pale worn faces, silently
preaching of temperance, and bidding us re-

member in our feasts "the vinegar and the
gall," uttering as it were that expostulation
of St. Bernard, "Quam sub spinoso Capite
delicatum est membrum !" while others, represented with the emblems that betoken
their respective celebrity, remind us of the
debt which the members of these Foundations owe to the Church and to the Country,
of which they so nobly payed their part and
we have yet to pay ours.

It is surely an office worthy of the character of these Foundations to exhibit to the
Country an example of simple habits and un-
artificial living. Here, if anywhere, an honourable testimony should be borne against the
spirit of a mammon-ridden age, and we should
be very jealous of any concessions being made
to it by the needless affecting of new fashions,
through which the luxury of a more wealthy
and self-indulgent time might creep into our
system and invade the strictness of our
rule.

> " Still may the spirit of the ancient days
> Rest on our feasts, nor self-indulgence strive
> Nor languid softness to invade the rule,
> Manly, severe, and chaste—the hardy school
> Wherein our mighty fathers learnt to raise
> Their souls to Heaven, and virtue best could thrive."[1]

This, however, has never been inconsistent with the exercise of a plain and primitive hospitality, " rem Deo et hominibus gratam," as write the compilers of Durham Chapter Statutes ; such as our Colleges have long been famous for, and to which services done to the cause of learning or the Church have always ensured a ready welcome. It is, moreover, in full accordance with the temper of our system that the successive terms of the year should bring round, as they do, their stated High-days and Feast-days, on which the splendid munificence of our Founders may be commemorated and exhibited with a becoming pride,—while at the same

---

[1] Faber's Poems, [p. 104.]

time it is fit, that their stated Vigils and
Fast-days too should not pass by unnoticed,
but our Colleges should bear, as they did in
George Herbert's time,[1] their public witness
to this much-neglected duty. " Indignus
quippe solemni lætitia est, qui statutam
vigiliæ abstinentiam non observat," writes
St. Bernard, in his Sermon on the Vigil of
St. Andrew, adding with a wonderful beauty,
" est autem universum præsentis pænitentiæ
tempus vigilia quædam solemnitatis magnæ,
et æterni sabbatismi quem præstolamur."
The student, such as I have [described him,]
is no stranger to this duty; he deems it
one which, while impressed by Scripture and
and the Church and the examples of the
Saints upon all, is especially binding on men
set apart to such purposes as are the mem-

---

[1] " In our publick halls, you know, is nothing but fish and
white meats."—G. Herbert's letter to Sir John Danvers,
speaking of the season of Lent. It seems from the same letter
that this was also the case on Wednesdays and Fridays.

bers of our College Foundations. For not to mention that here the commands and directions of the Church should find a scrupulous and willing obedience, abstinence has of itself a tendency to clear the intellect and elevate and unburden the soul; from whence it has been described as πτεροφυοῦσα τὴν ψυχὴν; and again, when used in the spirit of a Christian exercise, it has been said of it that, as "prayer is the wings of the soul, so fasting is the wings of prayer."

Now, if we read that the Priests of Egypt were so fearful that the body should not sit light upon the soul, that they were exceeding scrupulous about their diet, and would scarcely drink of the waters of the Nile, because they were thought to have a grossening[1] tendency, surely the Christian student should be gladly observant of this exercise of abstinence, were

---

[1] In the MS. this word is erased, but no other has been substituted. [Ed.]

it only as the "xerophagia" of a spiritual
athlete, to render, by God's grace, his soul
more alert, and more habitually master over
his body: and yet this is only one and by no
means the highest of the many uses of fasting.
Luxury indeed and self-indulgence are at all
times most unsightly in the seats of learning
and religion. "The very table of a monk,"
writes the great St. Basil, "ought to teach
even strangers sobriety and an unworldly
spirit;" and so too St. Bede, in his nervous
way, "Shall a man take the candle of his
spirit, to cover it under the bushel of glut-
tony, or hide it under the bed of sloth?"[1]
More especially unbecoming, however, would
they appear to be in our Colleges, where every
member of the Foundation is the Pensioner of
a private charity. Worthy to be remembered
in this view is the vigorous expostulation of
Bishop Fisher, that zealous and unwearied

---

[1] See Aurea Catena, St. T. Aquin. in St. Marc. c. 4. 21.

benefactor of the University of Cambridge,
written to Richard Crook, whom he had appointed Greek Professor after the departure of
Erasmus, but who proved unworthy of his
Patronage. He reminds him that to endow
the Foundation thus abused by him, he had
sacrificed what he might else have bestowed on
his own relations, and exclaims, " sed interim
stolidus eram, qui in tam ingratos pecuniam
expendi;" and then, after inviting him to
return to his duties as a lecturer, and his pro-
per attendance at the common table, which he
had neglected, accustoming himself to dine
with some friends in his own rooms, he adds,
" sed cave passurum me credas tantum offen-
sionis et exempli mali cujuslibet hominis
causâ intra Collegium." [1]

---

[1] See the original letter in Mr. Hymers' valuable appendix
to his new edition of the Funeral Sermon of the Lady Margaret, p. 210.

The very portraits of the old Founders that hang above him in the Hall would seem to the student to frown down upon him were he to waste their bounty on self-indulgence, or pervert it by indolence from the high and noble ends for which it was intended. He never hears the old Grace read without reverently joining in its beautiful prayer to the God of all Mercy, "that the gifts bestowed on us by our Founders and Benefactors may be used by us to His glory, and that with all who have departed in the faith of Christ we may rise again to eternal life, through Jesus Christ, Our Lord." How solemnly is the thought of the Resurrection of the body here brought into immediate contact with that of the daily provision for its support, as the true exorcism to drive away the spirit of intemperance. Very lofty and unearthly, again, is the tone of that other old Latin Grace, used in the Hall of Trinity

College, Cambridge, which closes with these
words :—

> " Mensæ cælestis participes
> Faciat nos Rex æternæ gloriæ.
> Sit Deus in nobis, et nos maneamus in Ipso."

There is indeed in almost all our ancient
Endowments a kind of visible connexion between the death-bed of the Testators and the
Statutes of their Foundations, which extends
a hallowing and religious influence to every,
even the lowest, part of these Institutions.

It was a pious and primitive custom, of
which the stone pulpits visible in several of
the ruined Refectories of our English Abbies
still exist as the memorials, which enjoined in
many of the old Monasteries, that the Scriptures or some holy book should be daily read
aloud to the Monks by one of the brethren
while they were at dinner.   This very ancient
practice is recommended in some of our older
College statutes; and the student is not un-
frequently tempted to wish it back again, or

at least those silent remembrancers such as scrolls inscribed with texts and mottos, with which the halls of our ancestors used often to be decorated: like as we read that the walls of the room in which St. Augustine dined were inscribed with a warning to the guests to refrain from maligning the absent.[1] Now that the check on unrestrained conversation provided by the requirement of the use of Latin has been entirely laid aside, he finds it good to bear in mind that wise saying of St. Thomas à Kempis, in his Vallis Liliorum, "Oportet ut sit valde ædificabile verbum, quod emendet silentium." [2]

One cannot but regret that this universal language which once distinguished and united the brotherhood of letters should

---

[1] See Tancredus, p. 368. St. Augustine inscribed on his table—
  "Quisquis amat dictis absentem rodere vitam
  Hanc mensam indignam noverit esse sui."—*Vit. L.* 4. 4.
[2] Vall. Lil. Opera, p. 552. Ed. Sommalii, 1625.

now have so entirely ceased to be spoken amongst us. There was something peculiarly grand and catholic in thus adopting one common tongue for the learned throughout Christendom, and seeking to remedy in some degree by this language of the fifth Empire, the dispersion of mankind at Babel. Moreover, our relinquishment of the use of Latin has contributed greatly, along with our insular position, to cut us off from intercourse with the Foreign Churches, and thus afforded another instance of the unforeseen consequences that may arise from ever so slight deviations from the laws of our Foundations. To take one more example, which will lead us back from this digression, it is in this way that we have lost the original meaning and intended benefit of that order of students called servitors or sizars, who once performed those offices in Hall which are now executed by menials, and were what the "lay brethren" still are in the convents of the Romish Church.

"It is easy to declaim," says Bishop Heber, in an admirable passage on this subject in his Life of Bishop Taylor, "against the indecorum and illiberality of depressing the poorer students into servants, but it would be more candid, and more consistent with truth, to say that our ancestors elevated their servants to the rank of students. And the very distinction of dress that has been so often complained of, the very nature of those duties which have been esteemed degrading, were of use in preventing the intrusion of the higher classes into situations intended only for the benefit of the poor; while, by separating these last from the familiar society of the wealthier students, they prevented that dangerous emulation of expense which has, in more modern times, almost excluded them from the University." The original character of this institution is now, as Bishop Heber most justly, I think, laments, quite altered; and "the want of such a frugal and humble

order of students is already felt by the Church
of England, as it eventually may be felt by the
nation at large." I have made this long quotation because I think it an example pregnant
with instruction as to the vast importance of
fully entering into and understanding the
spirit of our Institutions, before we venture
on passing judgment about even so appa-
rently indifferent thing as an article of
costume or a Rule about the serving of our
College Tables.

LECTURE ROOM.

LETTER VI.

LECTURE ROOM.

IN no place perhaps is the change that has
passed over our University system so
visible as in the College Lecture Room.
The very shifting of the scene from the large
Hall, with its various distinct groups of
students gathered round their lecturers, or
disputants engaged in practising for their
exercises in the schools, all under the eye of
one presiding superintendent, to the separate
room occupied by the Tutor alone with his
class of pupils, in few respects differing from
the scene of a Professorial Lecture, is itself
a type of this change. The College course

of instruction was formerly regarded solely
as preparatory or supplemental to that given
by the University Readers and Professors,
and the office of the Tutors mainly consisted
in accompanying their pupils to these public
Lectures, and to the Disputations and other
Exercises in the Schools. But now that the
Colleges have taken the office of education
and instruction almost entirely out of the
hands of the University (except so far as
the public Examinations still determine the
general character of the studies pursued), we
have the Tutor almost necessarily put into the
Professor's place, and his original office of
Guardian over his pupils almost thrown into
the shade by his more prominent functions
as their *Instructor*. On this has followed the
concentration in two or three members of the
College of those educational offices, which
were once dispersed among the great part
of the body of Fellows; and hence, with an
increase of *system*, a diminution of *personal*

influence and superintendence. Perhaps this latter change was a necessary consequence on the education of the under-graduates having passed out of the hands of the University Professors, in order to preserve that unity of teaching which is the great result aimed at in oral instruction. I am not now, however, passing judgment nor even suggesting changes, but I write to you here of what the system was, to enable you the better to understand that which has at present taken its place.

Many causes have contributed to bring this state of things about, and none so much as the gradual substitution of book study for that oral instruction which necessarily formed the staple of University education at a time when books on any subject were so few, and the copies of them so scarce and dear. A very great part of the present system of things in our Universities and Colleges is to be traced to the prodigious multiplication of books, originals as well as copies, during the last two centuries. The object of a College Lecturer now is mainly to guide and test your own reading and to supply its deficiencies. He has no longer to *supply* the *materials* of study, but to show you where to find them, to see that you do so, and to assist you in using and arranging them. The stores of knowledge, written and traditionary, which were once only to be obtained at the well-heads of the Monasteries and Universities, are now dispersed in innumerable channels throughout the country, but still the student needs living instructors: "Soul must catch fire through a mysterious contact with a living soul." "Mind grows not like a vegetable (by having its roots littered with etymological compost), but like a spirit, by mysterious contact of spirit; Thought kindling itself at the fire of living Thought."[1] Opinions will necessarily differ widely as to the

---

[1] Sartor Resartus, p. 109.

effects of this change. For myself I am
inclined to go a long way with the Egyptian
king in his judgment on the invention of
letters, given in the story, with which Plato
introduces his own deep thought on the
subject, at the end of the Phœdrus. The
knowledge we derive from books is perhaps
more accurate as to details, but it is less
retentively remembered, and less appropriated
and made our own, than that orally received.
It requires, we know, far less mental exertion,
—a much lower degree of attention,—to *read*
than to *listen;* and hence the majority of
readers, as Plato says, get to acquire with
readiness a variety of information without any
real instruction, a semblance of knowledge
without any knowledge at all, through the
neglect of exercising their minds, arising
out of their trusting to the external written
symbols and not rousing themselves to internal recollection. Besides,[1] another evil of

---

[1] See Prof. Sewell's Christian Morals, ch. 1.

books when used as a *primary* and *independent* mode of communicating knowledge, is that they have no power of explaining or adapting themselves to their different readers, and the system of private tuition so generally resorted to now at our Universities has arisen out of a general sense of this want of more personal oral instruction, which the original system supplied; and it cannot be put down, as some have proposed, without great injury, unless the general body of Resident Graduates, and especially the College Fellows, be restored to some of their original functions, by a greater subdivision of the work of education. The Professorial system can never supply its place.

I have spoken to you in a former letter of the salutary influence which the Collegiate foundations have exercised on the English Universities in the matter of *discipline*, but not less so has it been in that of teaching, by giving it a permanent Christian form. It has arisen out of the position of the Colleges in our two great seats of learning, that those who fill the Professorial chairs, and exercise the office of Instructors among us, are for the most part in Holy Orders. It is owing to them that the teaching, as well as discipline and government of the Universities, is in the hands of men bound by the most solemn of all ties to soundness of faith and holiness of life. It seems indeed probable that the Universities, as well as Colleges, had originally an ecclesiastical character, and that they first grew out of Cathedral or Abbey schools, taught by the Chancellor of the Church or others under his license; but at all events those of later origin have been purely literary and secular Institutions; and, had it not been for the foundation of Colleges, Oxford and Cambridge might now have been as little seminaries of religious education as are the Universities of Germany.

There are those who contend that the teaching of heathen literature, or instruction in philosophy or the sciences, are offices inconsistent with the high calling of a clergyman, and with which he ought to have nothing to do, forgetting that great truth which has been so eloquently expressed by a writer of our day, that "what man is amid the brute creation, such is the Church among the schools of the world; and as Adam gave names to the animals about him, so has the Church from the first looked round upon the earth, noting and visiting the doctrines she found there. She began in Chaldea, and then sojourned among the Canaanites, and went down into Egypt, and thence passed into Arabia, till she rested in her own land. Next she encountered the merchants of Tyre, and the wisdom of the East country, and the luxury of Sheba. Then she was carried away to Babylon, and wandered to the schools of Greece. And wherever she went, in trouble or in triumph, still she was a living spirit, the mind and voice of the Most High; 'sitting in the midst of the doctors, both hearing them and asking them questions;' claiming what they said rightly, correcting their errors, supplying their defects, completing their beginnings, expanding their surmises, and thus gradually enlarging the range and refining the sense of her own teaching." [1]

Various are the arguments by which it has been in this way attempted to bring about the legalizing, as it were, of the separation, which even now too commonly is made, between a man's intellectual and his moral being. Far different and more true-sighted was the wisdom which appointed "the service of the Chapel as the preparation for the service of the Lecture Room," and regarded the work of fashioning the souls of a generation by knowledge, as one too sacred to be entrusted to any but the ministers of the Christian Church. It formed part of that beautiful feeling with which the

---

[1] British Critic, lvii. p. 101.

98   LECTURE ROOM.

piety of old times regarded all who were
invested with the office of a Teacher or a
Prophet, which made them appoint that there
should be "world-honoured dignitaries and,
were it possible, God-ordained Priests, for
teaching;" — a feeling finely expressed in
those lines of the fervent Heathen Poet,

> " Dii majorum umbris tenuem et sine pondere terram
> Spirantesque crocos, et in urna perpetuum ver,
> Qui præceptorem sancti voluere parentis
> Esse loco."

When contrasting this with the shallow
views now so commonly held with regard to
this office, one might almost exclaim with
Tertullian, " O testimonium animæ naturaliter
Christianæ!" For more Christian-like surely
is their spirit, than that of an age which
would traffic with and so destroy the sacred
reverence belonging to this office, by setting
up the tables of the money-changers in our
very schools, which are or ought to be the
porches of our temples. In full consistency

with this maxim, the young student finds
himself in every part of the Collegiate system
regarded as a child of the Christian Church.
The most learned among her priests are entrusted with the charge of his education; and
the whole character of the place is essentially
unsecular. Each day's course is consecrated
by solemn prayers, and the subjects of his
studies are such as have reference to future
rather than present results; training his mind
by discipline, and teaching him the use of
weapons with which he is hereafter to make
conquests and win treasures. At the same
time we should remember what Cicero says,
at the end of his book "De Finibus:" "Ii
indocti, qui quæ pueris non didicisse turpe
est putent usque ad senectutem esse dis-
cenda."[1]   Four years are spent at College

---

[1] You will find some excellent thoughts on this subject in
a treatise of Mabillon's De Studiis Monasticis, a book well
worth reading, and full of thoughts extracted from writers on
these [topics].

in laying the foundation on which the future
fabric of knowledge is to be raised, and,
above all, in teaching that *science of method*—
of classifying and arranging our thoughts and
materials of thought—which arises from the
habit of contemplating not facts and things
only, but their *relations* to each other and to
ourselves. It is an admirable observation of
Coleridge's, in his chapter in "The Friend"
on this subject,[1] which I would warmly advise
you to read, that "the absence of method,
which characterizes the uneducated, is occa-
sioned by an habitual submission of the understanding to mere events and images, as
such, and independent of any power in the
mind to classify and appropriate them. The
general accompaniments of time and place are
the only relations which persons of this class
appear to regard in their statements." Now
this habit of mental arrangement and gene-

---

[1] Essay iv. sect. 2.

ralization it is one great object of those abstract sciences, which it will form part of your prescribed course of study, to convey; the object being not merely to store your mind, but to teach it how to make use of its stores. "We must show men" [it has been well observed] "that he who knows a little of many things can know much of none,— that it is deep knowledge, and deep knowledge only, which can command respect or ensure usefulness,—that power of mind, not accumulation of learning—faculties, not facts —are the real object of instruction, — and that this power is more a moral patience and control over the thoughts, than an instinctive readiness in combining ideas,—that it is dissipated and destroyed by indulging every caprice of thought, and by giving way to each temptation of knowledge instead of rigidly maintaining one definite course."[1]

---

[1] British Critic, No. 49, p. 205.

I do not however intend to dwell on the
systems of mental training pursued at our two
great Universities, and their respective or
comparative advantages; this has been very
sufficiently done already by many able hands.
I would however point out something of the
great benefit you will find in submitting your
own judgment, in a great degree, to that of
your College Superiors, as to the line of reading you should pursue and the Lectures you
should attend.   It is the fashion, doubtless,
among under-graduates to decry all lectures,
as interfering with private study, but you will
at once see that their standing ground is taken
up far too near the subject to allow them to
take a full and fair view of it.   Our young
students, for the most part, come up to College
fresh from a state of close discipline and a
system of compulsory studies.   They are here
in a kind of intermediate state, where they
have to learn the exercise of that inward principle of self-control in their pursuits, which is

to take the place of the external restraint they have just left. When this most wholesome lesson has been learnt, they will be then set free to choose for themselves the aftercourse they will pursue, but at present they are not left to ramble hither and thither, passing at will from one thing to another, in the wide field that lies before them. At this time of life the mind is like a mountain stream with an unsteady current, wearing for itself a bed, and so inclined to flow into any course already formed, so that if you do not avail yourself of that offered by the system of the place, you are only exchanging it for some chance and less safe influence. The College system gives abundant scope for the peculiar development of each individual mind, while it exercises just such a gentle restraining power as may image forth to it what inward Principle along with its own Experience is one day to supply. We are here to learn the great lesson that each man is not to be for himself " the measure of all

things;" that he is not at liberty to pick out
of the materials before him what he pleases
and arrange them as he will, but that there
are rules and forms after which all must build,
and from which none can depart with safety;
that there must be a centre of unity, external
to himself, to which all his studies must look.

Besides this there is a further advantage
arising from the course I am recommending,
which I can assure you, from experience, is
no slight one. When the student first enters
upon his College course he is usually accustomed to the having large masses of time on
his hands, and is seldom able to make the best
use of them. Here the hours of Lectures, as
also of Hall and Chapel, come in greatly to
his aid, subdividing his time for him into
manageable portions, and, if he rightly pre-
pares for each College exercise, imposing a
variety and succession in his studies which will
greatly prevent the danger of his flagging, and
which, in his first zeal, he is apt to neglect.

An attendance on the College Exercises and
and Lectures also, according to our present
system, involves the necessity of having con-
tinually to write down on paper what you
know in the subjects you are studying. This
a man will rarely do by himself, and indeed it
is scarcely possible to do so with profit, and
yet it is a practice of all others the most useful.
It is a trite but very true saying of Lord Veru-
lam's, " Reading makes a *full* man, conversation a *ready* man, writing an *exact* man."
There is nothing which tends to give an equal
clearness in thought and view, as this practice
of setting down on paper whatever you are
able on the subjects concerning which you
have been thinking or reading, for by this
means you directly learn how much you clearly
see and where the obscurity lies; and on these
two points, the perception of one's own acquaintance with, or ignorance about a subject
true knowledge much depends. Accuracy,
moreover, and accurate modes of thought,

that is the habit and faculty of grasping the *whole* truth on any subject, so far as you know it, and which, in the flourishing times of Greece, the Dialectic schools were intended to produce, are best arrived at by the practice of writing. This must supply to you now the absence of many of those University Dialectical exercises which, in the Middle Ages, when writing materials were scarce, were the sole test of knowledge, and indeed perhaps still [are] the surest and most trying.[1]

---

[1] The following extract from a letter of the Author's bears upon the subject of the great competition which exists in the University. It is in itself well worthy of insertion, and may help to relieve difficulties which some have felt. [Ed.]

"What you say of Cambridge has always been sadly true, all things make way for and look up to 'the Honors.' However, you are now in the dust of the course, and, having entered it, your duty is to run your hardest, not to outstrip this man or that man, but to 'calmly do your best' in the task which Providence has set before you. A man, called to be a soldier, may fight in a Christian temper: much more may one so read for Honors."

THE LIBRARY.

LETTER VII.

THE LIBRARY.

BOOKS are not now those scarce and dear things which they once were, when George Herbert "had to fast for it" when he bought a new volume.[1] There are few scholars now who cannot afford to read their favourite authors from copies of their own, and thus it is hard for us to appreciate the preciousness, nay rather sanctity, which a public collection of books possessed in the

---

[1] Letter to Sir John Danvers; the whole of which gives a curious insight into the difficulties which the dearness of books threw in the way even of a student so well off in the world as G. Herbert.

eyes of our forefathers, and in consequence
the jealous rules with which they guarded
the liberty of approaching it. But when we
know how that eighteen shillings was the
price of a printed copy of St. Jerome, in two
volumes, at Wynkyn de Worde's, (as we
learn from a bill of his to Bishop Fisher,)[1]
and the same of a copy of Origen, at a time
when £6. was the annual income of an
ordinary College Fellow, we may form some
idea of the straights to which the scholars
of those days must often have been put to
furnish themselves with books of any kind,
and the treasure which the possession of a
library must have been to them. Still it is
questionable whether these very difficulties
were not sometimes favorable to the development of truly thoughtful minds, just
as we know the powers of the memory were

---

[1] See appendix 4 to Hymers' edition of Bp. Fisher's
Funeral Sermon on the Lady Margaret.

then much more called out and exercised
than they are now. It would seem too that
in *early* times, when copies of the Holy
Scriptures were rare, while its truths were
not obscured, men were less in danger of
looking on the Word of God as a Book rather
than a Revelation, and so holding by its text
instead of its doctrines; of regarding it in
short as a Volume to be criticised, illustrated,
and argued out of, rather than an utterance
and voice of the Eternal Word to be listened
to, knelt before, reverenced, obeyed. How
piously does Thomas à Kempis speak in his
treatise called the Youth's Manual, of the
careful handling due to any book that treats
of holy things. " So take," says he in a
chapter about the care of a library, " so take
a book into thy hands to read, as just Symeon
took the child Jesus into his arms to hold
and embrace Him: and after thou hast done
reading, close the book and give thanks for
every word that proceedeth out of the mouth

of God, that thou hast found in the Lord's
field a hidden treasure. And let this treasure
of the Church, which has been brought to
light and elaborated by learned doctors, and
by good transcribers preserved, be carefully
kept from soil and decay." Such were the
feelings with which our Forefathers regarded
a Library; it was with them ground consecrated to the dead. And the student still,
whenever it is practicable, makes use of those
volumes which his ancestors have bequeathed
to his College, and in this point too recog-
nises the monastic principle of having all
things in common.

Books, however, of your own you doubtless must needs have, and a student takes
in few things a more pleasurable pride than
in seeing his shelves well filled. Let me,
however, recommend to you a degree of
watchfulness and self-restraint to the spirit
in which you collect them. There is a story
told of a monk called Zosimus, in the The-

saurus Asceticus of Possinus,[1] very beautiful
in this way, as illustrating the temper I wish
to commend to you. This good brother,
having a love for books, had given an order
to a famous and skilful Copyist for the transcribing of a Manuscript, but found on en-
quiring for it, that another Monk in the
Monastery, being struck with its beautiful
execution, had by a false pretence purchased
it, and got possession of it. The Copyist
urged Zosimus to compel this other Monk to
relinquish the Manuscript, but he only meekly
answered, "We get books to learn from them
love, humility, and gentleness; but if the
getting of them is to begin in quarrelling, I
had rather have none at all,"—an answer
worthy of a disciple of the great St. Basil.

The volumes of the College Library bring
more vividly before his mind the true nature
of all book-study, as a sort of solemn Descent

---

[1] 4to. Paris, 1604, διαλογ. xvii.

among the shades, where the rightly initiated
may hold converse with the spirits of their
Forefathers, and stand by in reverence, while
the great Dead, who once were the mighty
upon earth, pass before them. The privilege
of such high converse, however, is not to be
obtained by hasty and careless readers: the
golden bough must be sought out long and
painfully in the thick, dark wood, before we
can be admitted into the royal presence-
chamber of the departed. Such thoughts
are especially suggested by those old volumes,
where the footsteps of successive generations
of pilgrims are visible all through in the care-
fully-corrected errata written in neat quaint
characters on the margin; while the time-
stained, but unsoiled, pages show the pious
reverence which has been felt towards these
oracular shrines of the worthies of other times.
Or again, you may regard books in this light—
as the ruins and scattered monuments of antiquity, with their half-worn-out inscriptions,

from which we are to gather, as we may, a knowledge of the life of past ages. We may compare the literature of past and present times to a city (such as are several of our old Cathedral cities in England) of which, though much may be new, the greater part is perhaps one or two centuries old, while some of the buildings, especially the Churches, and the Cathedral itself, with here and there the scattered remains of some old monastic buildings once connected with it, belong to an elder time, reaching up to remote mediæval antiquity; and we may suppose further besides them, that there is still standing some octagonal tower, or ruined portions of the original city—embankments, which exhibit the vestiges of the old Roman colonists and soldiers.

Now the modern citizen may have dwelt for years among the antiquities of his native place, without ever having gathered from them, by putting together the scattered hints they supply, a single glance of insight into the

life which his forefathers lived there: he may
have stood beneath the solemn and lofty aisles
of his Cathedral, and gazed on the stained
windows, without reading in them a single
impress of the deep impulses and feelings
which raised them : or, again, he may take his
daily walk along the city ramparts, and among
the Roman remains which I have supposed
there, without so much as thinking of gaining
from them the least further view across the
distance which separates him from the times
of those ancient lords of the earth, or collect-
ing from their scattered fragments any notion
of the ancient form and appearance of his city.
He views for the most part whatever he sees
in the light of modern prejudices and opinions, and where these do not accompany him,
he sees nothing.

Now this is no exaggerated description of
the way in which very many readers content
themselves to live among books.   They are
accustomed either to look at the past through

the distorting glasses of modern notions, or else forget altogether their character as the speaking voice of men once alive like ourselves,—a proof that the Past still Is. They are like those painters who used to represent Scripture personages in Dutch dresses, picturing to themselves the facts of ancient times under a motley garb of modern associations and opinions.

Here at once the question arises, how are we to make use of the imperfect vestiges of older times, the precious monuments of the great and good who lived in them, which we possess in *books?* how are we to unite into harmony the scattered parts, and see them as they once existed in their prime?—how, in short, are we to *learn to read?* This is indeed a question of importance, more especially now that oral instruction has been so much superseded by book study, and this it is one main object of our Tutors and Lecturers to teach,— namely, the true way to read. The words of that historian, who penetrated perhaps more deeply than any before him into the obscurity that hangs over the past—I mean Niebuhr—will best express to you what I wish to say on this subject. He tells us that the object of his endeavours had been " to spread a clear light over this most interesting portion of ancient story, so that the Romans shall stand before the eyes of his readers, distinct, intelligible, *familiar as contemporaries,* with their institutions and the vicissitudes of their destiny living and moving." [1]　This is the way in which you should study ancient literature,—to draw from the brief notices and accidental hints contained in it, as much as you can of the daily *life* of the men of past ages, so as to be " familiar with them as contemporaries," only separated from us by an interval of space. We should look upon those whom we are reading about, or whose writings we are stu-

---

[1] [History of Rome, vol. i. p. 5.]

dying, not as the lifeless figures of the statue gallery, but as really *men,* with like feelings and passions as ourselves, though under different circumstances, and therefore differently developed. And for this end we should in some degree endeavour to work our mind into a resemblance of theirs, to throw ourselves into their position during the time we are studying them, and to try to *feel* with them : and this I believe to be the means by which we obtain real knowledge of anything, through the feelings, the heart, rather than the understanding. Seek to know their habits of thought, their familiar associations, the principles in which they grew up from their childhood, in what their early training consisted. These are a few among many points of investigation, which you will find of the greatest value in guiding you to the true principles and method of reading the writers of antiquity. By following this plan you will find obscure hints, which before were unintelligible, coming out into the vividness which they would have had to contemporaries; and, to return to our former illustration, the various ruins will group themselves together, and the Gothic Abbey or the Roman Fortification fill again with their old inhabitants, so that the Past will be for awhile again the Present.

I grant that for this a portion of that principle, which is by many contemptuously called enthusiasm, that is, self-forgetfulness in the love of your pursuit, is requisite; but this is only what Cicero has long ago said, when speaking of the study of oratory, that " without a zeal and burning affection, so to speak, nothing excellent in life can ever be attained,"—" studium et ardorem quendam amoris, sine quo in vitâ quidquam egregium nemo unquam assequetur."[1]

This is true of all pursuits, and perhaps more than any of the study of times gone

---

[1] Cic. de Orat. xxx.

by, where there must needs be an ardour to
carry you over difficulties, and to invest with
grace what must else seem uninteresting.
This principle will require of course to be
kept within due bounds, such as the calm
and holy Counsels read in Chapel will sufficiently point out to you; but under such
limits encourage it, for it is a noble one. By
trying to enter with energy into little things,
you will be able to do so in large; but at
the same time beware of dissipating this energy by letting it run into too many channels. Concentrate your powers on as few
objects as may be. "It would be well,"
writes Professor Sewell [1] in a passage which
I am sure you will thank me for transcribing
at large, "to impress upon young men of
the present day the value of ignorance as
well as the value of knowledge; to give them
fortitude and courage enough to acknowledge

---

[1] [British Critic, No. 49, p. 204.]

that there are books which they have not
read and sciences which they do not wish to
learn: and to make them feel that one of the
very greatest defects of the mind is want of
unity of purpose, and that everything which
betrays this betrays also want of resolution
and energy."

The student has a particular regard for
such books as have been the chosen companions of men whose memories he reveres:
considering that as it is in great measure by
book-study that we "build up the Being that
we are," so, by using the same moulds which
they used, we may hope to form in ourselves
something of the same character. Thus the
Catalogue given by Sir Thomas Herbert[1] of
the books which [formed] the daily occupation of King Charles, the Martyr, during his
confinement in Carisbrooke Castle, is not
without interest to him. These were, besides

[1] Memoirs. See Worsley's History of the Isle of Wight,
p. 119.

the Sacred Scriptures, Bishop Andrews' Sermons, Hooker's Ecclesiastical Polity, Doctor Hammond's Works, Villalpandus upon Ezekiel, Sandys' Paraphrase upon David's Psalms, Herbert's Divine Poems, Tasso's Jerusalem, (in Italian, with Fairfax's English Translation,) Ariosto and Spenser's Fairie Queen.

The student feels that indeed a book is a *living thing,* and accordingly is as heedful of the danger of evil communications in his reading as in his companions; knowing that the *spirit* in which a book is written is that which mainly remains with us, for good or evil, after we have read it.

"Sunt qui scire volunt, eo fine tantum ut sciant, et turpis curiositas est.
Et sunt qui scire volunt, ut sciantur ipsi, et turpis vanitas est.
Et sunt item qui scire volunt ut scientiam vendant, et turpis quæstus est:
Sed sunt quoque qui scire volunt, ut ædificent, et charitas est:
Et item qui scire volunt, ut ædificentur, et prudentia est."[1]

---

[1] St. Bernard, Serm. 36, in Cant.

COLLEGE FRIENDS.

LETTER VIII.

COLLEGE FRIENDS.[1]

THE years to be spent at College should be looked upon as an opportunity afforded for the formation of lasting friendships, to endure through life, and it may be beyond it. The age at which men usually go up to College is one in which there is a natural tendency to seek for something on which to lean the affections; the soul is then more especially like a vine in the spring-time, throwing out tendrils on every side, to see if perchance it may find some object round

---

[1] For much in this letter I am indebted to a young friend.

which to cling; and hence you will perceive
the great necessity of carefulness in the choice
of your friends, for in the present state of
your mind a very small bent may give a
permanent direction to its after-growth.

It often happens that persons of dissimi-
lar minds and character are drawn together
even by their very difference.   There is a
mysterious attraction in such cases which
draws together the Like and the Unlike,
resembling that which Philosophers tell us
exists between the positive and negative
poles of the magnet.   Very frequently, for
example, men of a naturally timid disposition will attach themselves to bolder and
more daring minds, finding a relief from their
own comparative irresolution in the presence
of minds more steady and unwavering: and
there is in these cases this other bond of
union, — namely the mutual admiration of
those qualities in each, which the other does
not possess.

But though such may live in intimacy even for a long time, still, as the author of "The Church of the Fathers"[1] observes, in the case of the energetic St. Basil and the sensitive, tender-hearted, St. Gregory, when their circumstances alter, or some sudden event comes to try them, very often the peculiarities of their respective minds will be brought into action, and what first led to intimacy may lead at last to difference and separation. Though we must not forget that even in these instances there must always be much in common both in taste and its object.

> " Facies non omnibus una,
> Nec diversa tamen, qualem decet esse sororum."

But in general we may say the *condition* of friendship is an *internal* principle of similarity, which, though it developes itself differently in different subjects, and is either checked or

---

[1] Church of the Fathers, p. 116.

K

brought out by accidental circumstances, *must* exist at base, if friendship is to continue. This it is which distinguishes a mere companionship from friendship. In the one case men are brought together by a similarity of *pursuit*, without regard to the *impulse* from which their several similar acts flow; in the other the *impulse* is for the most part the same. The first ground of union which you must seek in him who is to be your friend, is that you be agreed as to religion;[1] and many you may almost always find in College of congenial tempers with your own, with whom you may "take sweet counsel together and walk in the House of God as friends." But even one such is enough as your intimate bosom com-

---

[1] How deeply the Author felt this truth is shown by the following extract from a letter which he wrote a short time before he sailed for New Zealand, "one truth has come home to me very strongly on parting with so many friends, how unreal is all union of hearts that are not knit together in the bands of the Mystical Body." [Ed.]

panion, for there is truth in that old Greek proverb, οἱ φίλοι οὐ φίλος, — " he who has friends has no friend." Do not however be niggardly of your friendship : throw out your affections and sympathies generally and freely at this season of youth, when so many young warm hearts are gathered together from out all England, drawn towards each other by similarity of pursuits and common interests;— such a time for the meeting of kindred souls as life will never again offer. College, more- over, is peculiarly rich in such mutual associa- tions as especially form links of attachment between one man and another. To have knelt in the same Chapel, to have walked the same walks, read the same books, performed the same exercises, form a rich store of recollec- tions which, like a joint treasure, make the several owners as one.

To quote again the often-quoted words of St. Augustine : " Colloqui et considere, simul legere libros dulciloquos, simul nugari et simul

honestari, dissentire interdum sine odio, *tan-*
quam ipse homo secum, atque ipsa rarissima
dissensione condire consensiones plurimas :"—
such were the ties which bound St. Augustine
to Nebridius.

Remember how Bishop Ridley, in his "Farewell," which I have already quoted, speaks of
the friendships he had formed at Cambridge,
" where," says he, " I have dwelt longer,
found more faithful and hearty friends, received more benefits (the benefits of my natural parents only excepted) than ever I did
even in mine own native county wherein I
was born."

Do not then be niggardly in making and
accepting all such kindly proffers of love and
companionship, as may be a help, not a hindrance, to your studies and religious walk at
College, and as will form there one of your
purest sources of pleasure; but do not content
yourself with having many such companions,
without having also at least one friend. It

was the constant advice of good Dr. Hammond, to the young who came about him, "withstand the first overture of ill; be intent and serious in (what is) good; and be furnished with a friend;" and his biographer tells us that, in his apprehension, friendship was the next sacred thing unto religion; the union of minds thereby produced being, he judged, the utmost point of human happiness. [We may find in the "beloved disciple" the highest warrant and sanction for friendship; it is one which may suggest many deep and awful thoughts, investing, as it does, the love of man to man with a new and mysterious solemnity.[1]]

The lives of St. Basil and St. Gregory of Nazianzum form a beautiful example of a

---

[1] In the MS., among a few other pencil notes, occur the words "the beloved disciple." The Editor has ventured to express, in the text, the thought which they involve: for it would have seemed, to those who knew him, unlike the Author, had he passed by unnoticed this adorable pattern of friendship. [Ed.]

friendship, begun in the Academic Schools of
Athens, amidst the fostering influences of
common studies and mutual sympathies, and
an early ardour for piety and learning.

Nor is it only between fellow-students that
such lasting friendships have been formed at
College. The close intimacy that lasted
through their lives between Hooker and his
two pupils, Sandys and Cranmer, is a beautiful instance of the lasting and intimate connexion into which the ordinary relation of
tutor and pupil is capable of being raised; for
perhaps the office of private tutor in modern
times most nearly resembles that of Hooker
towards Sandys and Cranmer. The description which Walton [1] gives of it is too beautiful
to be here omitted. " Betwixt Mr. Hooker
and these his two pupils, there was a sacred
friendship; a friendship made up of religious
principles which increased daily by a simili-

---

[1] Walton's Lives, p. 179.

tude of inclinations to the same recreations
and studies; a friendship elemented in youth,
and in an University, free from all self ends,
which the friendships of age usually are not.
And in this sweet, this blessed, this spiritual
amity, they went on for many years: and, as
the holy prophet saith, ' so they took sweet
counsel together and walked in the House of
God as friends.' By which means they im-
proved this friendship to such a degree of holy
amity as bordered upon heaven—a friendship
so sacred that when it ended in this world it
began in that next, where it shall have no
end."

Take head against being supercilious. Most
men have something unpleasant about them
in their manner or look, or some deficiency
in taste, which, if we allow ourselves in
an extreme sensitiveness, will drive us from
their society. But we must not suffer this to
be, as it will produce self-isolation and self-
pride. You know I am not here recommend-

ing promiscuous or much company, but that,
as you are now in the mine, you should seek
for a friend as for a hid treasure.[1]

" Character," says St. Gregory, " is not at
once understood, nor except by long time and
perfect intimacy; nor are studies estimated by
those who are submitted to them in a brief
trial and by slight evidence."

There is another remark, which I would
make upon the subject of your friends, and
let me request you to weigh it well. Too
great freedom and familiarity are inconsistent
with any abiding friendship. That was a
most true saying which we find in the
" Golden Verses," πάντων δὲ μάλιστ᾽ αἰσχύνεο
σαυτὸν; far truer indeed, and in a far deeper
sense in the case of a Christian, than it was of
a heathen, for it is impossible for a Christian
to believe and live as he should do, without

---

[1] Extract from a letter of the Author's. [Ed.]

having a high reverence towards himself.
Now, viewing your friend as a second self,
such a reverence should you have towards
him. You ought to feel his friendship too
sacred a thing to trifle or take liberties with.
You must be content to see some things in
him which you do not yet understand, to
put up with some apparent uncongenialities.
Knowing that your impulses agree in the main
and are converging to agreement, when you
see things appearing irreconcileable to that
impulse, you must be content to wait; for,
says the Wise Man,[1] " Whoso casteth a stone
at the birds frayeth them away: and he that
upbraideth his friend breaketh friendship.
For upbraidings, or pride, or disclosing of
secrets, or a treacherous wound, every friend
will depart."

Besides which, the main difference between

---

[1] [Ecclesiasticus, xxii. 20, 22.]

the love of friend and friend, and that between husband and wife, seems to be that
in the latter case there is a moulding of
thought and feeling, so far as is possible,
into identity; in the former, the beings remain separate, each exercising a controlling
influence over the other.

FINIS.

JOHN THOMAS WALTERS, PRINTER, CAMBRIDGE.

For EU product safety concerns, contact us at Calle de José Abascal, 56–1°,
28003 Madrid, Spain or eugpsr@cambridge.org.

www.ingramcontent.com/pod-product-compliance
Ingram Content Group UK Ltd.
Pitfield, Milton Keynes, MK11 3LW, UK
UKHW012340130625
459647UK00009B/420